God is My Band-Aid

Phyllis Z. Brown

Illustrations by Susan Shorter

AuthorHouse™
1663 Liberty Drive
Bloomington, IN 47403
www.authorhouse.com
Phone: 833-262-8899

Because of the dynamic nature of the Internet, any web addresses or links contained in this book may have changed since publication and may no longer be valid. The views expressed in this work are solely those of the author and do not necessarily reflect the views of the publisher, and the publisher hereby disclaims any responsibility for them.

Any people depicted in stock imagery provided by Getty Images are models, and such images are being used for illustrative purposes only.
Certain stock imagery © Getty Images.

This book is printed on acid-free paper.

ISBN: 978-1-4918-1066-8 (sc)
ISBN: 978-1-4918-1067-5 (e)

Library of Congress Control Number: 2013915232

Print information available on the last page.

Published by AuthorHouse 09/29/2021

authorHOUSE®

Endorsement from Bishop Paul S.Morton

This book will be a blessing to many young people and anyone who reads it. As an educator, Phyllis Brown has a deep compassion and commitment to help young people reach their God-given potential. I am confident that this book will be used as a blueprint to help enrich the lives of our youth and aid them in their academic journey.

~Bishop Paul Morton,Sr.
Senior Pastor, Changing A Generation/ Atlanta, GA
Co-Pastor, Greater St. Stephen Ministries/New Orleans, LA

Presiding Bishop, Full Gospel Baptist Church Fellowship International

Hi my name is Kennedi!

I am so thankful you decided to read my book! This book is filled with God's promises which are designed to help when you are afraid, sad or in trouble.

As you read you will meet many of my friends who realized they could trust God's Word in the Bible Book and that it will make things better for them. Thank you for reading this book and my special prayer is that your faith and love for God will continue to grow BIG!

To my supportive and loving husband, thank you for being my best friend and all the shades of wonderful! To my three beautiful and successful children: Kaszia, Shaszda and Timothy, thank you for making my heart sing and to my amazing and adorable granddaughter, Kennedi Elyse, you are such a joy!

Dear God, there are times when I get hurt, times when I am sad and times when I am afraid.

I heard about the blessings and promises that are in the Bible Book that have been created to help me.

Thank you for making things better for me.

1

I am learning to ride my bike without training wheels but fell and scraped my knee, oooh weee that hurt me!

God's promises tell me that I can do ALL things with His help.

"I can do all things through Christ who strengthens me." Phillipians 4:13.

I am afraid of the thunder, lightning and rain.

Jesus said to fear not and He will keep me safe and cover me with His feathers.

"He will cover you with his feathers and under his wings he will be your shield and protection." Psalm 91:4

I want to raise my hand in class to ask and answer questions, but I am too shy.

God tells me to be STRONG and BRAVE.

"Be strong and courageous for the Lord your God will be with you." Joshua 1:9

I feel left out because I just moved to this country and I speak a different language in my class. It is hard for me to understand at times.

God said He will give me A LOT of wisdom and that He will help me understand.

"For the Lord will give you wisdom, knowledge and understanding." Proverbs 2:6.

My throat hurts really bad today and I can't stop coughing.

God's promises tell me that He can make my throat feel better and will heal me fast.

"I cried to the Lord and he healed me." Psalm 30:2

Today my family and I are moving and I am going to a new school tomorrow. I sure hope I meet new friends.

God's promises tell me if I am happy in Him my prayers will be heard and answered.

When someone bullies me at school it scares me but God promises to protect me.

* Important- Always tell your parent, teacher or an adult when you are bullied.

"The Lord is my helper, I will not be afraid what man can do to me."
Hebrews 13:6

My mom says it is my responsibility to clean my room every day. I have clothes and toys everywhere and it is too much to clean.

God says that I have to obey my parents in EVERYTHING and when I do, it will make Him happy.

"Children obey your parents in everything for this pleases the Lord."
Colossians 3:20

Children are a heritage from the LORD,

offspring a reward from him.

Psalm 127:3

New International Version (NIV)

Order a copy and contact information-

Phylliszbrown.com

Authorhouse.com

Amazon.com

Barnesandnoble.com

Printed in the United States
by Baker & Taylor Publisher Services